# Crock

**Teddy Butler Copeland**

# Living
## in a
# Pressure
# Cooker
# World

# Crock Pot Pot Living in a Pressure Cooker World

## 13 Lessons to Help Turn Down the Heat

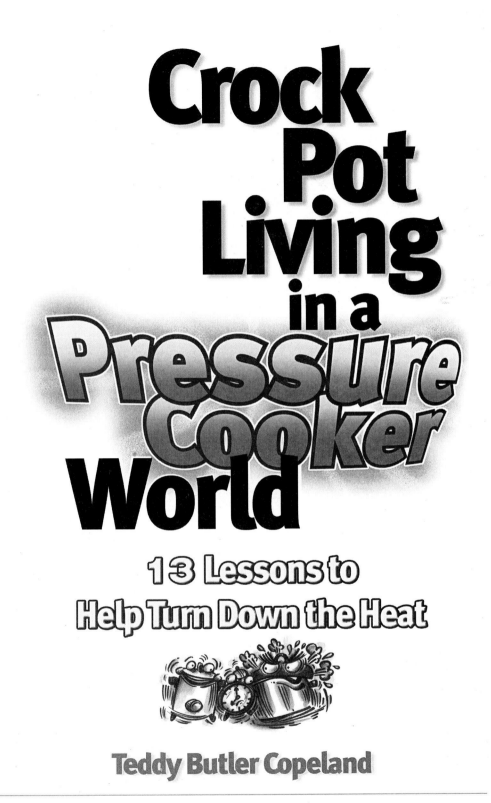

## Teddy Butler Copeland

## 13 Lessons to Help Turn Down the Heat!

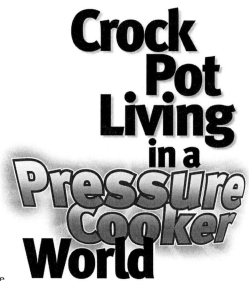

# Crock Pot Living in a Pressure Cooker World

Lambert Book House
4139 Parkway Drive
Florence, Alabama 35630

© 2007, Lambert Book House

I have in my files numerous items with no point of reference and whose original usage I was unable to trace. Thus, I extend my apologies for any illustrations not adequately documented.

Published by
**Lambert Book House**
4139 Parkway Drive
Florence, Alabama 35630

ISBN 978-0-89315-417-2

Printed in the United States of America

# Contents

**pressure cooker** n: an airtight utensil for quick cooking or preserving of foods by means of superheated steam under pressure.

**crock pot** n: an electric cooker (i.e., slow cooker) that maintains a relatively low temperature.

# Me and the Monster

Remember pressure cookers?

I do. Growing up, the steamy, noisy monstrosity was a fixture in our Alabama kitchen. My mom used the pot to speedily cook meats or preserve homegrown vegetables, and quite possibly to keep me in line. (Not really. But she could have! Let's face it: a pressure cooker was a scary thing to a kid. The commotion it created was greater than me, my sister, and all our cousins combined.)

More than once, when Mom got sidetracked and forgot it, our pressure cooker made everyone pay. There would be a loud explosion (only slightly below sonic boom level), followed by liquid spraying everywhere—on walls, floors, and ceilings. Pinto Bean Brown was hardly a Sherwin Williams color choice.

Even on good days, the pressure cooker made its presence known. It created new dances on the stove top, whistling and hissing, forcing me to scream into our wall phone so my best friend could hear me over its racket (not a good thing in the secret-sharing elementary days). The monster shook cabinets and rattled my fillings. I took to cowering in the den, a safe distance from spewing range.

Fortunately, by the time I left home for my very own kitchen—and my very own wall phone—a new cook's helper was arriving on the scene.

In 1970, the Rival Company acquired the assets of Naxon Utilities Corporation and, with them, rights to its "Beanery" slow cooker. A year later, society's very first crock pot was introduced.

This remarkable new super hero product — avocado green, naturally — became one of my favorite wedding presents. (And it might as well have retained the "Beanery" moniker as far as we were concerned, since that was our main fare on a $15-a-week grocery budget!) Still, it couldn't have been more perfect for a novice chef struggling to put her husband through graduate school. The crock pot cooked all day while I was at work, standing firmly on the counter top. Best of all, it made no sound whatsoever. And an added bonus: there were no Pinto Bean Brown walls.

So what on earth do cooking utensils have to do with life styles?

Nothing, really. Then again, everything.

Slow versus fast is a contrast as old as the fable of the tortoise and the hare. Granted, the majority of the time, speed gets all the accolades. But as Old Testament writings point out, the race is not always won by the swift (Ecclesiastes 9:11). Sometimes slower is better. Often times, slower is best.

Never has this reminder been more needed than in our 21st century world. Look at us: We have an entire industry (fast food) catering to our hurry-scurry schedules. DayTimers keep track of meetings and appointments too numerous to fit into the square of a calendar anymore.

but eliminated, greedily absorbed by educators eager to put youngsters on the "fast track," teaching more, sooner.

Our lives today are like my mother's pressure cooker: too noisy, too active, always on the verge of blowing up!

As this book will suggest, we would do well to replace scenes of mounting pressure with a slower and simpler regiment.

We must learn to turn down the heat. Remember, the tortoise fared well with a steady, relaxed pace. Yet, the Bible gives numerous recipes/axioms for letting off the pressure.

# Introduction

A lady was giving a party for her granddaughter. She had gone all out with a caterer and a band, had even hired a clown for entertainment. Just before the party was to start, however, two fellows showed up on her doorstep. Down on their luck, they asked for some assistance. Feeling sorry for them, the woman said she would feed them a meal if they would go out back and chop her some wood. Gratefully, they headed to the rear of the house.

Meanwhile, guests began to arrive, and the party seemed to be going well. But then the woman got a phone call from the clown, saying he was stuck in traffic and would not be able to make it after all. She was very disappointed and did not know how on earth she was going to keep the children entertained. About that time, she looked out the window and saw one of the fellows in the backyard doing cartwheels. She watched in amazement as he swung from tree branches, did midair flips, and leaped high into the air.

She called out the back door and said to the fellow chopping wood, "What your friend just did is absolutely marvelous! I have never seen anything like it. Do you think he would consider repeating his performance for the children at the party? If so, I would be willing to pay $50."

The man said, "I don't know, but I'll ask him." Turning to his friend, he said, "Hey, Willie, for $50, would you chop off another toe?"

This, I think, is the way we are in our pressure cooker world. We run around doing all these incredible things, but it may be more out of desperation than anything else.

My prayer is that the thoughts in this book will help you. May we all learn better how to deal with life and accomplish our goals without chopping off our toes in the process!

Apply the principles of this little book bit by bit. I am convinced if you do, you will eventually see results.

# Chapter 1

# *Take It Easy, You Will Last Longer*

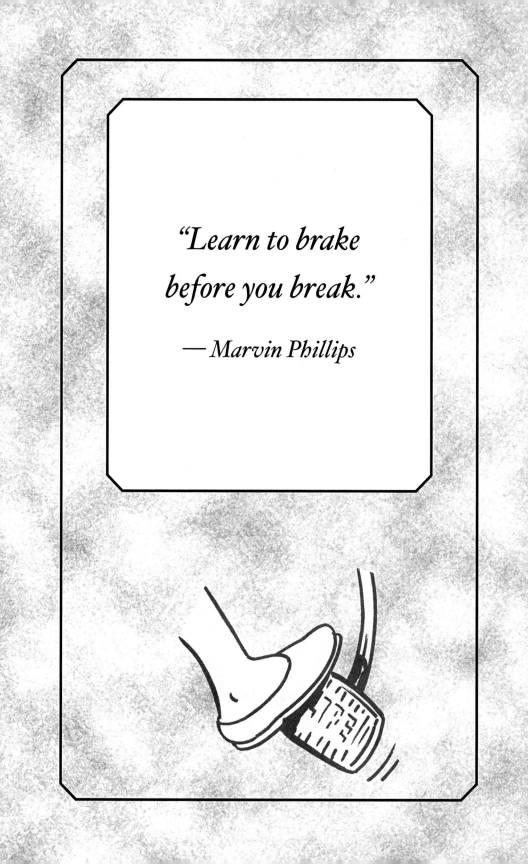

*"Learn to brake
before you break."*

— *Marvin Phillips*

## Take It Easy, You Will Last Longer

Peter Marshall, the late preacher and U.S. Senate Chaplain, told a story in one of his sermons that bears repeating.

There was a fellow who, with his father, farmed a little piece of land.

Several times a year, they'd load up the ox-cart with vegetables and drive to the nearest city.

Except for their name and the patch of ground, father and son had little in common.

The old man believed in taking it easy . . . and the son was a go-getter type.

One morning, they loaded the cart, hitched up the ox, and set out.

The young fellow figured that if they kept traveling all day and night, they'd get to the market by next morning.

He walked alongside the ox, and he kept prodding it with a stick.

"Take it easy," said the old man. "You'll last longer."

"If we get to market ahead of the others," said his son, "we have a much better chance of getting good prices."

The old man pulled his hat down over his eyes and went to sleep on the seat.

Four miles and four hours down the road, they came to a little house.

"Here's your uncle's place," said the father, waking up. "Let's stop in and say hello."

"We've lost an hour already," complained the go-getter.

"Then just a few minutes more won't matter," said his father. "My brother and I live so close, yet we see each other so seldom."

The young man fidgeted while the two old gentlemen gossiped away an hour.

On the move again, the father took his turn leading the ox.

By and by, when they came to a fork in the road, the old man directed the ox to the right.

"The left is the shorter way," said the boy.

"I know it," said the old man, "but this way is prettier."

"Have you no respect for time?" asked the impatient young man.

"I respect it very much," said the old man. "That's why I like to use it for looking at pretty things."

The right-hand path meandered through woodland and wild flowers.

The young man was so busy watching the sun sink he didn't notice the lovely sunset.

Twilight found them in what looked like one big garden.

"Let's sleep here," said the old man.

"This is the last trip I take with you," snapped his son. "You're more interested in flowers than in making money."

"That's the nicest thing you've said in a long time," smiled the old fellow. A minute later he was asleep.

A little before sunrise, the young man shook his father awake.

They hitched up and went on.

A mile and an hour away they came upon a farmer trying to pull his cart out of a ditch.

"Let's give him a hand," said the father.

"What, and lose even more time?" exploded the son.

"Relax," said the old man. "You might be in a ditch some time yourself."

By the time the other cart was back on the road, it was almost eight o'clock.

Suddenly a great flash of lightning split the sky. Then there was thunder. Beyond the hills, the heavens grew dark.

"Looks like a big rain in the city," said the old man.

"If we had been on time, we'd be sold out by now," grumbled his son.

"Take it easy," said the old gentleman. "You'll last longer."

It wasn't until late in the afternoon that they got to the top of the hill overlooking the town. They looked down at it for a long time. Neither of them spoke.

Finally the young man who had been in such a hurry said, "I see what you mean, Father."

They turned their cart around and drove away from what had once been the city of Hiroshima.

Are we hurrying to Hiroshima? Are we living such high-pressured, fast-paced lives that we're on course to destroy ourselves and our families and quite possibly lose our souls?

Like the profit-minded son in the story, we must be reminded of the benefits of a slower journey. We need to take the time,

> Rest in the Lord, and wait patiently for him: . . .
>
> — *Psalm 37:7* (KJV)

make the time, to enjoy the beauties of nature and the blessings of family. We need to experience the rejuvenation that comes from rest and the satisfaction that comes from unselfishness.

## The Fourth Commandment

Do some study on the Old Testament Sabbath. The word we often think of in connection with Saturday actually means "rest."

Why do you suppose rest was one of the commandments given on Sinai? Do you think God knew that man would resist taking care of himself?

A good resource is Rick Atchley's *Sinai Summit.* Let's consider the following points he makes in a chapter entitled "Distress Signals."

❖ The Sabbath was a safeguard to remind the Jews that there was more to life than work. Do we need that reminder today?

❖ The Sabbath was just as important, perhaps more so, during the busiest of times, in both planting and harvesting seasons. It was not something to be done just when it was convenient. Yet when our schedules are tight, don't we have a tendency to let spiritual matters slide?

❖ The Sabbath was a sign to other nations. It helped non-believers see that the Israelites prospered not because of the industrious nature of the people, but rather because of the goodness of their God.

❖ The very first Sabbath was God's (read Genesis 2:2,3). In the narrative for the first six days of creation, there is always the phrase, "And there was evening and there was morning, the _____ day." Yet there is no closure to the description of the seventh day. Many take this to mean that God's rest has never ended, and that we as Christians can look forward to someday sharing the rest He now enjoys (Hebrews 4:9-11).

Or course, the difficult part is learning to do so. If we do not enjoy resting with God now, do we expect to enjoy resting with Him eternally?

### Exercise

Choose a place you can go
for solitude.

It may be on a deck
in early morning hours
or behind locked doors
in a bubble bath.

Make a resolution to escape there
at least twice a week.

## Scriptures

Exodus 14:10-29

1 Kings 20:40

Psalm 46:10

Isaiah 30:15

Isaiah 32:17

Matthew 11:29,30

Mark 6:30-32

# Chapter 2
# All Stretched Out

*"The solitude you crave
today may be
the noise you
miss tomorrow."*

## "All Stretched Out"

In her book, *Scribbles: Sketches for Stressed Out Moms,* Cindy Dagnan tells about shopping in a large discount store one afternoon amidst throngs of other harried customers. With her was her elderly mom and two young daughters. As she tried to maneuver her cart down a crowded aisle, another shopper paused right in front of her, blocking the passageway. Pressed for time and mentally running down the list of all she still had left to do that day, Dagnan shifted her weight from one foot to another and unconsciously rubbed the back of her neck. Suddenly her youngest daughter stood up in the buggy and shouted to the offender, "Would you please move? My mom is getting all stretched out!"

While she did not quite have the terminology correct, this little girl undoubtedly had picked up on the tension and time pressures of modern life styles.

My friend Trina has two young sons. When the smallest, Dustin, was just a newborn, they had experienced a trying day. The baby had been fretful, and everything that could possibly go wrong had. Trina asked Daniel, her five-year-old, if he would like to stop by his favorite fish place and pick up some dinner. His eyes grew wide. "Of course," he replied, excitedly. Then he added, "Maybe a hushpuppy will calm my nerves!" (Trina says if that were the case, then she needed about a dozen!)

What does it say about today's society when even our children feel the exhaustion and effects of stress? A more sobering question might be: Where have they learned it?

## Definitions

The word stress originated from another, similar word: *distress*, which means a dangerous situation or peril. We are all familiar with the dilemma of a ship in distress.

Hurried lives can lead to that same sinking feeling.

Webster defines stress this way:

1) *A physical, chemical or emotional factor that causes bodily tension and may be a factor in disease causation. 2) A state resulting from a stress; one of bodily or mental tension resulting from factors that tend to alter an existent equilibrium.*

Thou wilt keep him in perfect peace, whose mind is stayed on thee: because he trusteth in thee.

— *Isaiah* 26:3 (KJV)

In other words, something that causes tension is stress, and the result it produces is also stress.

Note, first of all, the fact that stress can lead to health problems. In the 1920's and 1930's, Harvard had a physician-researcher named Dr. W. B. Cannon. Dr. Cannon discovered and developed what came to be known as a human body's "emergency response" reaction.

According to his research, whenever people feel that they are in some sort of danger, physical or mortal, numerous changes take place inside them. Pupils dilate, blood pressure increases, digestion and other so-called "non-essential activities" slow down, and adrenalin glands start to pour out adrenalin. Production of other hormones intensifies as well, as the body prepares either to fight or flee.

Now this is great if your house is on fire and you need to get out in a hurry, or if someone is seriously injured and you must go for help. However, those who experience high levels of stress in their lives stay in this state of emergency continually, and this is not good. Such panic-induced production takes its toll on the body. With all this wear and tear, individuals become much more susceptible to hypertension, ulcers, migraine headaches, and even heart disease.

The second part of the definition emphasizes that stress can alter our equilibrium. On a recent trip to the bank, I noticed my favorite teller had displayed a small plaque at her booth. *One complete year of perfect balancing!* it boasted. I marveled at the accomplishment. Harmony in financial dealings is admirable, but its challenge pales in comparison to the difficulty of maintaining balance in our lives.

According to an automobile mechanic, a car wheel with even a small amount of imbalance, say seven ounces, produces a tremendous amount of pressure (up to 13 pounds!) on a wheel when it is spinning at 50 miles per hour. Go faster, and the pressure continues to increase.

Now in a car, we know that can eventually ruin the tires. In life, however, damage caused by imbalance is even more difficult to repair.

## The Great Chase

Two state troopers were chasing a car east on the Interstate one day. They were right on his bumper and almost had him when the suspect crossed the state line. As soon as the driver did that, the first trooper pulled over on the side of the road and parked his vehicle. The rookie trooper pulled in right behind him, jumped out, and asked, "Hey, Sarge, why did you stop?"

The sergeant shook his head and replied, "Don't you know? He's in another state now, and they're an hour ahead of us, so we'll never catch him!"

I know that feeling. Don't you? Not of being in a car chase, but of thinking that there is no way I can ever catch up. I experience it quite often; most of us do. There never seem to be enough hours in a day. And because we rush around in high gear, trying to do so much, we end up feeling very stressed.

## Supermarket Etiquette

I left the grocery store in a hurry. Rather, I tried to leave in a hurry.

But a little man stood in my way. He paused near the exit, counting his change deliberately, caressing the worn bills and tenderly tucking them into a thin wallet. He rearranged the plastic bags in his cart methodically. Finally, he began edging toward the door. Obviously, he had time to spare.

I, on the other hand, had places to go and things to do!

Still, supermarket etiquette prevented my passing him. At least until we got out of the store. Then, of course, I whipped by, leaving him in a flurry of dust. As I screeched out of the grocery store parking lot, I noticed he had yet to make it to his car.

It dawned on me, looking back in my rearview mirror, that a slower pace of life is typical of two age groups: older folks and children.

Our oldest son, Adam, attended a small Brazilian preschool in our neighborhood when he was four. Our younger son, Luke, would walk with me to meet him every day at lunch. It was only a few blocks from where we lived, but it took forever to get there because Luke, age 2, had to stop and look at every crack in the sidewalk. Pick up every stick. Examine every rock. Hide in every doorway.

Somewhere between childhood and old age, we lose that fascination with life.

What a shame.

## Lessons From Lamaze

My babies were born in the 1980's, smack dab in the midst of the natural childbirth craze. ("Craze" is an appropriate term because most older women assured us we'd lost our minds to consider childbirth without anesthesia.)

A couple of things from my pregnancies have stayed with me (Well, three if you count all the stretch marks). Both were relaxation procedures emphasized in the Lamaze training classes we took. To my surprise, I found the exercises beneficial for moments other than labor and delivery.

The first involves proper breathing. Deep cleansing breaths, we were taught, were essential before and after contractions. Guess what? They're important in any time of stress. Pay attention the next time you get keyed up about something. More than likely, you will find yourself taking rapid shallow breaths, involving only your chest. Force yourself to draw two or three of the doctor's-office style, slowly sucking large amounts of air into your lungs and puffing out your belly as you inhale. Increased oxygen can trigger longer, calmer brain waves, the kind that lead to general relaxation. (Warning: too many deep abdominal breaths, of course, will cause you to feel dizzy.)

The second involves choosing a focal point to get your mind off the immediate discomfort. This may be a peaceful place you can imagine, a pleasant memory you recall or even a soothing phrase you repeat.

"Repetitive actions like chants are a way of getting yourself into a meditative state—or near enough to help you relax," says Dr. Esther M. Sternberg of the National Institute of Mental Health.

What chant could be better than a favorite Bible verse? To make them even more meaningful, try personalizing key references. (For example, John 3:16: For God so loved ME, that He gave . . . or Isaiah 40:31: If I wait on the Lord, He will renew my strength . . .).

Talk yourself through a difficult moment or, better yet, using words from scripture, let God talk you through it.

**Exercise**
Go to a thesaurus and look up
all the synonyms
for the verb *relax*.
Write down three of your favorites.
If you did these things,
how would your life
(or at least the quality of it)
be changed?

## Scriptures

Psalm 18:6

Psalm 25:4

Psalm 39:6

Psalm 120:1

Proverbs 17:1

Isaiah 40:30,31

1 Thessalonians 4:11

# Chapter 3

# *Things That Increase the Pressure*

*The job that produces*
*the most stress, hands down,*
*is always said to be that*
*of an air traffic controller.*
*But mothers can do*
*the job of three*
*air traffic controllers*
*with ease on any given day!*

## Things That Increase The Pressure

What causes stress in your life? Country singer Shania Twain describes a day to which most of us can relate:

> The car won't start, it's falling apart
>
> I was late for work and the boss got smart
>
> My panty line shows, got a run in my hose
>
> My hair went flat (man, I hate that!)
>
> Just when I thought things couldn't get worse
>
> I realized I forgot my purse
>
> With all this stress, I must confess
>
> This could be worse than PMS!

Obviously stress can be brought about by serious, monumental problems in life. More often than not, however, its source is something relatively minor.

Dealing with automated phone systems, for example. How frustrating is it to spend fifteen minutes trying to get through to a live person? Or maybe you cannot find your car in a parking garage. What feeling of helplessness tops that? Perhaps you have misplaced the one item of significance in a week's stack of junk mail. Or you are stuck in a traffic jam when you are already running late.

Then again, it could be a personal battle, like struggles with weight. A woman once confided, "Stress for me is when my fattest fat pants don't fit!"

I love the story about a lady who had lost close to 50 pounds and was cleaning out her closet. She pulled out a pair of slacks that she had not worn in quite some time.

"Wow!" she exclaimed, looking them over. "I must've been 180 when I wore these!" Her young niece, visiting at the time, looked up from her toys. "How old are you now?" she asked.

Sometimes, in this regard, we get caught in a vicious cycle because it is so tempting to look to food to relieve our stresses. After all, stressed is desserts spelled backwards! I used to have a little magnet on my refrigerator that said, *There's nothing in life that can't be handled with prayer and chocolate!* (How many of us turn to the chocolate before we turn to prayer?)

For many, stress comes from the workplace. A lady with the same occupation as me—church secretary—told about someone coming up to her after services and saying, "It must be wonderful to work in a stress-free environment!" We both had a good laugh over that. Pardon me if I shatter some illusions here, but working in a church office is not a stress-free environment! If you don't believe me, show up on a day when the copier breaks down, you have got a stack of mail outs that have to go, and some little lady calls to complain about the hymnbooks being too heavy! I love my job, but it can be trying at times, just like most every job.

Another area that can cause stress is family relationships. A man came into work one morning looking very depressed. "What's wrong?" a co-worker asked. "My wife and I had words this morning," he explained. "I had some, but never got to use mine."

Then there are kids. Someone asked a harried woman with four energetic offspring, "If you had it to do over, would you have children?"

"Sure," she replied. "Just not the same ones!"

Parenting in the early years can be very stressful as you have to help with homework, chauffeur children back and forth to activities, supervise baths, and serve as referee/arbitrator between siblings. But guess what? It does not get any simpler as they get older. I have a cartoon in my files that shows a teenage girl in a department store. As she is paying for a skirt, she says to the cashier, "Can I return it if my mother likes it?" Sometimes when kids are trying to establish their own identities and become independent, it seems like regardless of parents' opinion on a topic, they are going to go the opposite way. And that is frustrating.

For most folks, the biggest source of stress gets back to our pace of life. "I feel like I'm being pulled in seven different directions at once," one woman said. "There's just not enough of me to go around!"

> This *is* the day *which* the Lord hath made; we will rejoice and be glad in it.
>
> — *Psalm* 118:24 (KJV)

Most females can relate to that. You see, we try to be Superwoman and do it all.

Remember a song from the feminist movement that said, "I am woman, hear me roar?" For most of us, it is more like, "I am woman, hear me gasp!" I have a sign on my computer at work that sums it up pretty well:

*I am strong. I am invincible. I am tired.*

## How Heavy

A lecturer asked his audience, "How heavy is a glass of water?" Answers ranged from 20 to 500 grams. The lecturer replied, "The actual weight doesn't matter. It depends on how long you try to hold it. If you hold it for a minute, that's not a problem. If you hold it for an hour, you'll have an ache in your arm. If you hold it for a day, you may have to call an ambulance. In each case, it's the same weight, but the longer you hold it, the heavier it becomes. You need to put it down and rest before holding it again."

The same is true with our burdens.

Do not carry your stresses of the day home with you. Put them down. You can pick them up again in the morning after you have rested.

— Anonymous

# *Why?*

The sound of wild geese flying home
Awakened me tonight.
What is it guides them when they roam?
Who taught them form of flight?
What is it tells them when to go
Their north or southward way?
How is it that they seem to know
To go without delay?
I watched their silver wings tonight
Against the darkened sky
And marveled at their ordered flight
And stopped to ponder why.

If they can trust their Maker's plan,
Then why can't we, the sons of man?

— Author Unknown

## Exercise

Matthew 6:27 asks a very
pointed question.
What does worrying really
accomplish?
Make a list of the things
you worry about.
Then, transfer your list to little
squares of paper
(one worry per square).
Pray over your worries,
then ceremoniously rip
them to shreds
and dump them in the garbage can!

## Scriptures

Psalm 55:22

Psalm 56:8

Proverbs 12:25

Matthew 6:25

2 Corinthians 4:17

Philippians 4:6

1 Peter 5:7

# Chapter 4

# *How We Got Here*

*Lost time
is never found again.*

*— Benjamin Franklin*

# How We Got Here

When did things get so crazy?

There was a time when families ate meals together instead of in shifts.

There was a time when people knew their neighbors.

And there was a time when busyness was not equated with success.

According to Tim Kimmel, in just a matter of a few decades, we have gone from *Little House on the Prairie* to *Little House on the Freeway.*

> We are the instant generation. We like to tell a sign behind a restaurant what we'd like for dinner and then expect the people inside to have it prepared by the time we pull our car around to the serving window. We can cut projects down to the wire because we know we can ship a package anywhere in the continental U.S. (and now abroad) within twenty-four hours.

Automatic tellers give us instant cash. Microwave ovens give us immediate meals. Modern malls give us sudden debt.

Sociologists say the shift began back in the days when families first moved out to the suburbs. Fulfilling the so-called "American Dream," they purchased that Brady Bunch ranch-style house with a two-car garage. Of course, then they needed a second car to go in that garage; so to pay for the car (and the new home), husbands began to work overtime or wives got a job.

With more money coming in, of course, there ended up being more to spend. So spending became a national pastime, one that most Americans mastered (and they have the cards to prove it!). Madison Avenue marketers presented tempting portrayals of what everyone wanted and convinced them it was a necessity.

In the meantime, new technology entered the scene. Air conditioning kept children indoors more; television (and later, video games) became their chief means of entertainment. To replace old-fashioned backyard ball and neighborhood games, organized sports stepped up to the plate.

Parents, eager to provide their children with more advantages than they ever had, began enrolling them in every type of activity imaginable, from art classes to ballet lessons to traveling (and sometimes year-round) sports teams.

> Wait on the Lord: be of good courage, and he shall strengthen thine heart: wait, I say on the Lord.
>
> — *Psalm* 27:14 (KJV)

Even women who did not work outside the home began to feel the crunch. *If I'm a stay-at-home mom,* noted a bumper sticker in the 80's, *why am I always in my minivan?*

With more places to be and more activities to squeeze into a day, rush hour went from being a description of 5:00 traffic to an around-the-clock reality for most families.

As a result of moving at such break-neck speed, patience became a quality bordering on extinction.

Based on a recent Associated Press article by Calvin Woodward, most people these days get antsy after five minutes on hold on the phone and fifteen minutes max waiting in line. Grocery stores are the place they most hate to wait, he says, but the Department of Motor Vehicles is not far behind.

"If you ask the typical person, do you feel more time-poor or money-poor, the answer almost always is time-poor," says Paco Underhill, whose company Envirosell monitors the behavior of shoppers and sellers across the U.S.

"We walk in the door with the clock ticking with various degrees of loudness in our heads. And if I get to the checkout and if I have the perception it's not working efficiently, often that clock gets even louder."

Unfortunately most folks do not understand how they arrived at this predicament, and they do not have a clue how to change it.

"I must like this frantic pace," one mom says, "because if nothing is going on, then I plan something! If I see a lull or empty spot on the calendar, I find something to fill it. It's almost like I don't know how to act if I'm not stressed."

## Modern Times

There is a famous scene from an old Charlie Chaplin film, *Modern Times,* where Chaplin is standing next to a conveyor belt. As beautiful, creamy cakes roll by, he sprays on frosting, adds a rose or two, then puts the cake in a box, and places the box on a shelf. Everything is going well, and he appears to be quite pleased with himself.

But then the belt is cranked up to a higher speed. In the rush to keep up, things get crazy. Cakes fly by, icing gets sprayed all over the place, and the finished products splatter, one on top of each other, on the floor.

You may have seen a similar routine on *I Love Lucy* reruns where Lucille Ball stuffs her mouth and shirt full of chocolates, trying to stay caught up.

There was a time we used to really laugh at scenes like these, but they are not quite as funny as they used to be. Why? Because they represent what we live nowadays: life on the accelerated conveyor belt. We move at a pace equal to the comediennes, and the acceleration takes its toll.

Remember that old slogan: *The hurrieder I go, the behinder I get?* Though it may have some grammatical issues, it contains a lot of truth. The more we rush, the more things tend to pile up on top of us.

Yet we are the ones controlling the conveyor belt! Remember Abraham Lincoln's statement, "Most folk are about as happy as they make up their minds to be?" I am convinced that most folks are as busy as they want to be. Our schedules are a matter of choice.

Please remember that you are not an employee of a mass production company striving to meet or exceed a quota. In your life, recognize that quality is better than quantity.

Slow things down.

You can.

You should.

And when you do, I guarantee, you will be glad you did.

**Exercise**

Everyone has a "To Do" list these days.
Why not make a list of
"Things **Not** To Do"?
Post it in a prominent place, and be sure
to include the following:

— worry

— get uptight

— over commit myself needlessly.

## Scriptures

Proverbs 23:4

Micah 7:7

Matthew 6:28-31

1 Timothy 6:17

Hebrews 13:5

James 5:1-6

# Chapter 5

# *Who's In Charge, Anyway?*

*"When I wake up in the morning,
I reach for my Bible.
I check to see if Romans 8:28
is still there.
If it is, I get up and go about
business as usual.
But if I ever check and
it's not there,
that'll be the day
I just go back to bed."*

*— Richard Rogers*

## Who's In Charge, Anyway?

For years, my husband and I have gotten together sometime during the Christmas holidays with a group of eight to ten couples. We take turns hosting the party, and it is always great fun. Last December, for example, I made my dessert, bought my gifts for take-away (we always play Dirty Santa), and went. It was a blast.

The previous year, however, the scenario was a little more complicated. Why do you think that might be? You guessed it: the party was at *my house*. Did I get a little more stressed about it than normal? You bet I did! I drove myself—not to mention other family members—crazy, trying to have everything Goldilocks-style (*just right*).

Elaborate decorations were hung, tables were arranged, and games were planned. Whew! It was both exhausting and nerve-racking. I felt totally responsible. I was *in charge*.

Sometimes, I think we approach life with this same attitude. We knock ourselves out, worrying and fretting, thinking everything depends on us.

But we are wrong.

You see, when it comes to life, we are definitely not the ones in charge.

Jeremiah 10:23 says, "It is not in man who walks to direct his own steps."

A friend of mine who used to live in California was at a Los Angeles Dodgers baseball game one day with her husband and their four sons. She had the youngest son (around three years old at the time) in the ladies' room with her. As she finished up, he slipped out of the stall to wash his hands. Imagine her panic when she heard a little voice say, "I'm through, Mommy. Bye!" Needless to say, she could not get of there and after him fast enough! Can you imagine a little boy trying to find his way back to his seat by himself in a place like that? It would be impossible. But it is equally impossible for us to maneuver through the mazes of life on our own, without God's guidance.

> The God of my rock; in him will I trust: he is my shield, and the horn of my salvation, my high tower, and my refuge, . . .
>
> — 2 *Samuel* 22:3 (KJV)

One of my favorite passages is Psalm 31:14,15, which says, "But as for me, I trust in You, O Lord; I say, You are my God, my times are in Your hand."

In her book, *Disciplines of the Heart,* Anne Ortlund recalls the following incident:

> My brother Bobby and I used to play marbles on our living room rug. He always won, but I was a sucker, and we'd keep playing until Mother called us to dinner.
>
> We never thought to ask each other, "Do you think we'll get any dinner tonight? Do you think

Daddy brought home any food? Do you think Mother cooked it? What if they've forgotten us? What if they've decided not to feed us any more? Should we have done something to earn it, so they'd keep giving it to us?"

Hey, we were their *kids*. Our job was to play marbles, and their job was to supply the grub!

When we get overly anxious in life, stressed and frazzled from all there is to do, we need to remember we are not the one in charge.

God is.

## Just The Two of Us

How much time do you have alone? Probably not much, if you are a mother of young children (unless you lock yourself in the bathroom from time to time).

How much time do you have alone with God?

In the hymn *My God and I*, I. B. Sergei describes the kind of relationship we need with our Maker:

> *My God and I go in the fields together,*
> *We walk and talk as good friends should and do;*
> *We clasp our hands, our voices ring with laughter,*
> *My God and I walk through the meadow's hue.*
> *He tells me of the years that went before me,*
> *When heavenly plans were made for me to be;*
> *When all was but a dream of dim conception,*
> *To come to life, earth's verdant glory see.*
> *My God and I will go for aye together,*
> *We'll walk and talk as good friends should and do;*
> *This earth will pass and with it common trifles,*
> *But God and I will go unendingly.*

So many of the things we rush around doing fall into the category of "common trifles." Time alone with God takes our focus off those stresses and puts it on what really matters: things that are eternal.

## He's Got The Whole World In His Hands

I remember learning in school that two-thirds of the earth is covered with water. That amazed me. In fact, I almost found it hard to believe. In my North Alabama hometown, far from the coast, it seemed to me there was much more land than water.

Once I moved overseas, however, my perspective changed. During the six years our family lived in Brazil (and in subsequent visits back), we did a lot of flying over the Atlantic Ocean. Looking out my porthole window at what seemed like an endless expanse of sea took my breath away.

So did the concept of Isaiah 40:12.

*"Who has measured the waters in the hollow of his hand . . ."*

Several years ago, my cousin's wife gave birth to a premature baby who weighed a mere nineteen ounces. Precious little Kenya lived six weeks and was so tiny she literally fit in her daddy's palms.

If our God has the whole world in His hands, and we know He does, then I should rest assured. Certainly He is able to take care of the little corner of it that I call my own!

## A Sanctuary

When I was in college, I worshipped at a little congregation out in the country called Refuge. And that is exactly what it was. It was a peaceful place to go, offering comfort and respite from the daily drudgery and difficulty of college life. It was out of town, off the beaten track, in a beautiful, serene setting.

Do you need a place like that? A place where you will be taken in, loved, and accepted?

I know just the place. It is in the loving arms of God! He is to be our "dwelling place."

When people ask me where I live, I respond automatically, giving our subdivision's name. I quote an address. That is my *physical* place of abode. But the real place I stay, my true shelter, should be the Lord.

## No Matter What Happens

Legend has it that for a Cherokee youth's rite of passage, his father takes him, blindfolded, into the forest and leaves him alone. He is required to sit on a stump the entire evening and not take off the blindfold until morning. No matter what happens, he cannot cry out for help. Once he survives the experience, he is considered a man.

During one such episode, the Indian youth involved was terrified. Wild beasts were all around him; they seemed to be getting closer. The wind blew wildly. Hours passed ever so slowly.

Finally, the horrifying night came to an end. The sun appeared, and the boy was able to remove his blindfold.

It was then that he saw—on the stump next to him— his father, who had been watching over him the entire night.

Though he did not realize it, he had never been alone.

And neither are we.

Don't be afraid, God tells us in Isaiah 41:10. He will strengthen us, help us and stay with us through the dark, lonely nights.

## Exercise

Read Psalm 91:1-10 every day this week. Pray the following prayers:

*Monday*—Thank God for being your fortress.

*Tuesday*—Thank God for being your place of refuge.

*Wednesday*—Thank God for protecting you.

*Thursday*—Ask God to help you make Him your dwelling place.

*Friday*—Ask God to help you begin each day with calmness.

*Saturday*—Thank God for the clamor in your life, which means you have an important place in the lives of so many!

## Scriptures

Psalm 9:9

Psalm 36:7

Psalm 46:1

Psalm 59:16

Psalm 62:7

Psalm 91:1-7

Joel 3:15,16

# Chapter 6

# *I Need A Little Space*

*"The moment you wake up
each morning, all your wishes
and hopes for the day
rush at you like wild animals.
And the first job each morning
consists in shoving it all back;
in listening to that other voice,
taking that other point of view,
letting that other,
larger, stronger, quieter life
come flowing in."*

— C. S. Lewis

## "I Need A Little Space"

The first few years of my husband's life, he lived with his parents in Chapel Hill, North Carolina, while his dad was going to school at North Carolina State. When Roger was three or four, he was playing hide and seek one day with some little friends. In the course of the game, he discovered what looked like a great hiding place. He found some metal steps leading up to a door, and they were hollow on the inside. Perfect, right? He opened them up and crawled inside.

You may be able to guess what happened next. Even though Roger was relatively slim at the time, he got stuck inside. There was not enough room for him (maybe explaining why he has bouts of claustrophobia!).

It is a panicky feeling when you do not have enough space, isn't it? Sometimes in day-to-day life, that same sentiment may creep in. It is as though the world is closing in on you because you have so many things to do, so many demands, so much responsibility. Mentally you begin to feel as though you can barely breathe.

What can you do when that happens?

One solution is to follow the advice cited in modern relationships that get too serious too soon. Give yourself some "space." Back off a bit. Take a little time.

Put some distance between you and the source of your stress.

Often, by doing that, you will get a much clearer perspective of things.

Once when our children were young, Roger came in from work, and I began immediately to complain to him about my day. I said, "You won't believe what happened. I had just finished folding this huge stack of laundry, and Luke came along and messed it all up!" Luke was about three at the time, as I recall. It was a load of whites, and he had grabbed all the panties and hung them on his ears and stacked boxers on his head! Do you know what my sweet, sympathizing husband said in response to my dilemma? Not, "Oh, you poor baby, you had to fold it all over again." No. He said, simply, "I wish I could have seen that." I will never forget his comment. It cured my aggravation, and made me realize what a blessing it was to be at home with my children all day long and see the cute, precious—and, yes, exasperating!—things they did.

> By the word of the Lord were the heavens made; and all the host of them by the breath of his mouth.
>
> —*Psalm* 33:6 (KJV)

Granted, one-on-one parenting of young children day in and day out can be stressful. So when things start closing in on you, and you find yourself ready to climb the walls, hire a babysitter or trade out with a friend who also has little ones. Get away for an afternoon. Go out on a date with your husband. What happens? Usually you will end up missing your kids, anxious to get back home to them.

By backing away just a bit, you may be reminded that the thing causing you so much stress, in reality, is a wonderful blessing.

Traffic: Is it not awful at times? But would you really want to go back to horse and buggy days?

Household chores drive you bonkers; you just cannot seem to get ahead. (It has been said that when a man does dishes, it is called helping. But when a woman does dishes, it is called life!) Still, would you trade your living quarters for the house your grandmother called her own?

A job may be trying and exhausting, hard on your nerves. But how many unemployed or disabled workers would welcome such a position, stresses and all?

Most of us have heard of the renowned scientist, Alexander Fleming. Working at St. Mary's Medical School in London in the 1920's, Fleming put off cleaning up his lab so long that a blue mold began to grow on the dishes. That mold, come to find out, could cure bacterial infections. Fleming's discovery—penicillin—eventually won him the Nobel Prize.

We may not find a miracle in the midst of our messes like Fleming did. But I guarantee, more often than not, there is something special in every stressful situation if only we will look close enough to see.

## "My Lucky Day"

Garland Chapman of Midland, Texas, tells a story that happened during his days as an elementary school principal.

A little second grade boy had a rather eventful day. It started out in the morning when he fell from the bus and hit his head on the concrete, requiring three stitches.

At recess, he and another student ran together, knocking two of the little boy's teeth loose and bruising his lip.

That same afternoon, he fell and broke his arm.

The principal decided he better just take him home before anything else could go wrong.

On the drive, he noticed the youngster was clutching something in his hand.

"What do you have there?" he asked.

"A quarter," answered the little boy.

"Where did you get it?" the principal asked.

"I found it on the playground," he replied. "You know, Mr. Chapman, I never found a quarter before. This is my lucky day!"

*There is something to be excited and thankful for in every day, even one filled with misfortune and catastrophe.*

## Attitude Is Everything

A woman woke up one morning, looked in the mirror, and noticed she had only three hairs on her head. So she said, "I think I'll braid my hair today." She did, and she had a wonderful day.

The next day, she woke up, looked in the mirror and saw only two hairs on her head. "Hmm," she said. "I think I'll part my hair down the middle today." She did, and she had a wonderful day.

The next day, she woke up, looked in the mirror and had only one hair on her head. "Well," she said, "today I think I'll wear my hair in a pony tail." She did, and she had a wonderful day.

The next day, when she woke up and looked in the mirror she did not have a single hair on her head. "Yea!" she exclaimed. "I don't have to fix my hair today!"

Attitude is everything.

## Exercise

Speaking of space, go outside one night and look up at the stars. Take a blanket and sit for a while.

Read some of the passages in Psalms that talk about the heavens. Meditate on the fact that God made our universe. What does this tell us about His power?

Sometimes, looking at all the space out there makes us feel small and insignificant. But Psalm 147:4 says God knows each star by name. Imagine how He feels about those of us made in *His* image!

## Scriptures

Job 9:7,8

Job 26:7

Psalm 19:1

Psalm 127:4,5

Psalm 139:7-12

Psalm 147:4

Colossians 3:15

# Chapter 7
# *Where Does the Time Go?*

*"The real secret of
how to use time
is to pack it as you would
your luggage, filling up the
small spaces with
small things."*

*— Henry Haddow*

# Where Does The Time Go?

A first grade teacher had gathered her students around her and was going to teach them to tell time. Using a conventional clock, she said, "Boys and girls, today we're going to learn about the hour hand and the minute hand."

One of the little boys in her class interrupted her at this point. "I don't need to learn how to tell time on that kind of clock," he said. "My daddy bought me a digital watch."

Looking down at his wrist, he paused a minute, then reported brightly, "Right now, it's 10 minutes to 38!"

That young fellow needed a lesson on time more than he thought he did. And we, with our busy schedules and rat race life styles, should consider some thoughts about time ourselves.

First of all, remember that our time here is limited.

Time, as we presently know it, began when Adam and Eve sinned back in the Garden of Eden. That was the point when death entered the world. Before sin, there had never been a need to measure time because it was never ending. Today, our time on earth has a beginning and an end.

Yet, we tend to forget that, don't we? We think we are going to live forever, or at least we certainly act that way. (And we are going to live forever somewhere—just not here on this earth!)

When I was 17, my first cousin died. I did not know a lot as a teenager, but one thing I saw clearly through the tragedy our family experienced: there is no guarantee of time.

Because of that, we need to use our time wisely.

Someone has calculated a schedule that compares an average lifetime with a single day, beginning at 7:00 in the morning. Here is what it says:

> If your age is 15, the time is 10:25 a.m.
> If your age is 25, the time is 12:42 p.m.
> If your age is 35, the time is 3:00 p.m.
> If your age is 45, the time is 5:16 p.m.
> If your age is 65, the time is 9:55 p.m.
> If your age is 70, the time is 11:00 p.m.

I was a bit disheartened after reading that. It is past 5:00 in the day for me! The bulk of my time is already past. Which brought to mind the question: How have I spent the time I have had?

To every *thing there is* a season, and a time to every purpose under the heaven:

— *Ecclesiastes* 3:1 (KJV)

I am reminded of the quote by Ben Franklin: "Does thou love life? Then do not squander time for that is the stuff life is made of."

Realizing that our time here is limited will encourage us to make the most of it (Ephesians 5:16), using it for things of consequence.

Realizing our time is limited will also cause us to treasure the time we have.

Ecclesiastes 3:11 says that God has made everything beautiful in its time. There are so many wonders in God's creation. We need to be aware of them and slow down enough to enjoy them.

We also need to appreciate whatever phase of life we happen to be in at present. If you are pregnant, enjoy it. If you have toddlers, try to get some rest, but enjoy it! If you are in the empty nest or retirement years, enjoy the unique opportunities and blessings that come at that point in life.

The late Erma Bombeck has a classic piece that helps us to remember the importance of savoring the moment.

> *One of these days you'll shout, "Why don't you kids grow up and act your age?" And they will. Or, "You guys get outside and find yourselves something to do . . . and don't slam the door!" And they won't.*
>
> *You'll straighten up the boys' bedroom neat and tidy . . . bumper stickers discarded . . . spread tucked and smooth . . . toys displayed on the shelves, hangers in the closet, animals caged. And you'll say out loud, "Now I want it to stay this way." And it will.*
>
> *You'll prepare a perfect dinner with a salad that hasn't been picked to death and a cake with no finger traces in the icing and you'll say, "Now there's a meal for company." And you'll eat it alone.*
>
> *You'll say, "I want complete privacy on the phone — no dancing around, no pantomime, no demolition crews. Silence! Do you hear?" And you'll have it.*

*There'll be no more plastic tablecloths stained with spaghetti, no more bedspread to protect the sofa from damp bottoms, no more gates to stumble over at the top of the basement steps, no more clothespins under the sofa, no more playpens to arrange a room around.*

*You'll have no more anxious nights under a vaporizer tent, no more sand on the sheets or Popeye movies in the bathroom, no more iron-on patches, wet knotted shoestrings, tight boots, or rubber bands for pony tails.*

*Imagine a lipstick with a point on it, no babysitter for New Year's Eve, washing only once a week, seeing a steak that isn't ground, having your teeth cleaned without a baby on your lap, no PTA meetings, no car pools, no blaring radios, no one washing her hair at 11:00 at night, having your own roll of transparent adhesive tape.*

*Think about it. There'll be no more Christmas presents out of toothpicks and library paste, no more sloppy oatmeal kisses, no more tooth fairy, no giggles in the dark, no knees to heal, no responsibility.*

*Only a voice crying, "Why don't you grow up?" and the silence echoing, "I did."*

## All the Time in the World

God is not like us. (Thank goodness!) But we tend to forget that. Sometimes I think we assume He is in as big of a rush as we are and that He does not have the time to bother with us. That is so far from the truth.

Several years ago a little girl was traveling with her family by train. Her mother had put her to bed in the top bunk of a compartment, but it was dark and she was afraid. Every little bit, she kept calling out, "Mother, are you there? Daddy, are you there?" They assured her they were, but every few minutes she repeated the question. Finally, a man trying to sleep in a nearby compartment, called out, "Little girl, would you please be quiet and go to sleep?"

The little girl was quiet for a moment and then whispered, "Mother, was that God?"

Unlike that gentleman, God does not ever get tired of hearing from His children. Remember in the Garden of Eden when He asked Cain, "Where is your brother Abel?" He already knew the answer, but He wanted to hear it from Cain. He wanted Cain to come to Him, to confess and to pour out his heart.

It is beyond our limited mind to understand how God is available to us every hour of every day, ready at our beck and call to listen. One little boy wrote this letter: Dear God, when is the best time I can talk to you? I know you are always listening, but when will you be listening *extra hard* in Troy, New York?

God listens extra hard to his children around the clock. He has no time constraints.

# Spreading Your Music
# Throughout the Day

Author and lecturer John Erskine said that at 14 years of age, he learned his most valuable lesson about time.

Erskine's music teacher was quizzing him about how often he practiced the piano. He replied that he always tried to play his pieces at least an hour a day.

Instead of the praise he expected to receive, however, the woman surprised him by saying, "Oh, don't do that."

"When you grow up," she explained, "time won't come to you in long stretches like that. Do your practicing in minutes wherever you can find them—five or ten before school, a few after lunch, or between chores. Spread it throughout your day, and music will become a part of your life."

Erskine later went on to apply this same principle to his own writing.

Nearly all of *The Private Life of Helen of Troy,* his best known work, was penned on streetcars on his daily commute!

# The Devil Invented
# Permanent Press

Not really. An elderly woman did claim that once, however. "I used to pray when I did my ironing," she explained. "Now that I don't have to iron as much, I find myself praying less."

I am not much for ironing either. (In fact, when a friend's mom tripped over her ironing board and broke her leg, I told her that proves what I have always suspected—ironing can be hazardous to your health!) Still, there are other tasks I am compelled to do that occupy my hands only and leave my mind free to converse with the Father.

Using time wisely is an art. It is also a biblical principle; Paul encourages us to "redeem" the time (Colossians 4:5).

My youngest daughter plays collegiate soccer and spends a lot of time training. She came home the other day from an outing with a friend, all excited about a prospect she had not considered before. Her friend's grandmother, she told me, spends twenty minutes a day walking on a treadmill, and she uses that exercise time to pray over a lengthy list of family and friends. "I'm going to start praying when I work out," Bethany said with determination.

Busy as we are, we all have spaces in our days we can fill with things to help us in our Christian walk. An added bonus: we will end up more in tune with our Maker.

### Exercises

Listen to tapes or CDs of praise music or inspirational messages. You can do this when you are in your car or if you are out jogging.

Occasionally, turn the radio off and experience that very rare commodity of silence. Meditate or pray.

Have good Christian literature on hand to pick up at home when you have a few extra minutes.

Carry a small modern-day translation of the New Testament in your purse to read if you get stuck in traffic or have to wait at the dentist's office.

## Scriptures

Ecclesiastes 3:1-8

Ecclesiastes 8:6

Ecclesiastes 9:11

2 Corinthians 4:17,18

Ephesians 5:16

Colossians 4:5

James 4:14

# Chapter 8

# *The Original Harried Homemaker*

"The morning is the gate of the day and should be well guarded with prayer. It is one end of the thread on which the day's actions are strung and should be well-knotted with devotion. If we felt the majesty of life we should be more careful of its mornings. He who rushes from his bed to his business and waiteth not to worship is as foolish as though he had not put on his clothes or cleansed his face and as unwise as though he had dashed into battle without arms or armor. Be it ours to bathe in the softly flowing river of communion with God, before the heat of the wilderness and the burden of the way begins to oppress."

— Charles Spurgeon

## The Original Harried Homemaker

Her name was Martha. Her story is recorded in the New Testament, Luke 10:38-42.

Put yourself in those pages for a minute. Imagine you are her.

You live in an obscure little village on the outskirts of Jerusalem. More than likely, you are a widow, in charge of a household that includes your brother Lazarus and your sister Mary.

One day—maybe it was a busy day, with laundry to do and figs to preserve—unexpected visitors drop by. Jesus is at the door with twelve tired, dusty disciples. Right at lunchtime.

What do you do? How do you feel?

Remember, there are no fast food restaurants nearby, so you cannot send Lazarus out for chicken. Telephones have not been invented yet, so you can not order pizza. Good thing you have those casseroles in the freezer, right?

Or maybe that was not the scenario at all. Maybe you knew ahead of time that Jesus was coming by with some of His followers. Oh, what plans you make! Everything has to be just perfect. You clean the house till it shines and plan an elaborate five-course meal. You make endless trips to the marketplace. Only the finest for the Master! There is so much to do, you become frantic. With one eye on the clock (well, maybe the sundial), you race around checking items off your list, exhausted, impatient, a nervous wreck.

Sound familiar? Have you ever been so busy gathering up your visuals for a Sunday school class, putting the finishing touches on food for a potluck, getting the kids into clothes they hate, that you snap somebody's head off?

One woman overhead her little girl say, "Well, you can tell it's Sunday morning by the way Mom is screaming!"

This chaotic tizzy has become the norm for every day of our lives—not just Sundays. For that reason, probably no story in the Bible speaks more directly to women in the twenty-first century than does this story in Luke 10.

By looking closely at Martha, we take a look at ourselves.

Notice, first of all, that she had a lot of good qualities.

*She was hospitable.* She received Jesus into her home and from all indications was delighted to have Him there. No booking a room at the local inn. She welcomed Christ, along with the large group that inevitably accompanied Him.

*She was organized.* She knew what needed to be done, and she set about not only to do it, but to enlist the aid of others.

*She loved Jesus.* What she was doing, she was doing for Him. But still, the Lord chided her, rebuked her. Why? What does this story say to us today?

First of all, it says that attention to Jesus is the most important thing in life.

What should have top priority is not how clean one's house is, what is for supper, or whether or not all the chores are done. It should be concerns of the soul.

Life should always be lived against a backdrop of eternity. Nowadays, everywhere we turn there are statistics on various things. Well, consider this statistic: One of out every one person dies. Pretty sobering, is it not?

Several years ago, my cousin's wife, who was pregnant at the time, watched a televised news program about Sudden Infant Death Syndrome. She did not realize that her five-year-old was paying any attention to it, but a few days later he asked, "Mommy, are we going to get one of those quick-dying babies?" We may not like the thought, but let's face it, we are all quick-dying. Whether we live a few days or a hundred years, our lives are but a moment in comparison to eternity.

Since that is the case, we would do well to follow the instructions in Matthew 6:33 and seek first God's kingdom.

Now you may say, "Oh, but, Teddy, I do that! Why, you would not believe how involved I am at my church. I do this . . . and this . . . and this . . . ."

Oh, I believe it. I am the same way; many of us are. We rush around just like Martha. But activities for God are not necessarily the same thing as a relationship with Him.

There is an interesting passage in Hosea 4:6 where the prophet says, "My people are destroyed for lack of knowledge." That verse always stumped me. Had the Israelites not heard of God? I wondered. How was that possible? I thought they were His people! Did they not study the scrolls hard enough, not memorize all the shalls and shall nots? That was not it at all. In Bible times, the word "knowledge" carried a different connotation than the intellectual, factual kind of knowledge we are familiar with today. It was the word used to describe the close, unique sharing between a husband and wife. Hosea is not saying that the people had not heard of God; he is saying they did not have an intimate relationship with Him. Oh, they were still going through the motions—offering sacrifices, doing acts of service—but their hearts were far from Him.

If we are not careful, the same thing can happen to us today. We may assume we are putting God first when we are busy with a lot of activities.

There is a sad story told about a man whose wife died suddenly. He was left alone and brokenhearted to raise their precious young daughter. When the first holiday season rolled around, he decided to take a week off from work and spend it with the little girl. How he anticipated their time together! On the first day, however, when he arose, he found that the little girl had locked herself in her room and would not come out until supper time. Every day that week was the same. Finally, Christmas morning rolled around, and under the tree was a package wrapped in newspaper and tape with layer after layer of ribbons. Triumphantly, the little girl offered it to her father. He opened it and inside found a pair of hand-knitted socks. "That's what I was working on so hard every day in my room," she explained. The father gathered her up in his arms. Tears rolled down his cheeks. "What's wrong, Daddy?" the little girl asked. "Don't you like the socks?"

"Of course I do," he replied. "I love them. But what I really wanted was just to spend some time with you."

Does God ever shed tears over our activities, our mad flurry to do what we think He needs, longing all the while just to spend a little time with us? Isaiah 65:1 says, "I was ready to be sought by those who did not ask for me. I was ready to be found by those who did not seek me."

Secondly, the story of Martha tells us that outward things do not impress the Lord.

I can just imagine Martha being all caught up in what tablecloth to use and whether or not to break out the good china. What should she serve as her main dish, what vegetables, what dessert? Did Jesus care about those things? No, it did not matter.

What do you think was Jesus' favorite food? Have you ever wondered? Was it fish? That is what He cooked and served the disciples on the beach after His resurrection in John 21. Some Bible commentators speculate that Jesus is almost playful in Luke 10:42 when He says Mary has chosen the "good portion."

Come unto me, all *ye* that labor and are heavy laden, and I will give you rest.

— *Psalm* 118:24 (KJV)

Martha is preoccupied with food and dishes and what to serve next and when, and Jesus seems to say, *The best dish of all—the one I like the most—is what your sister is doing!*

Do you catch all the implications? It is as if He tells her, *I don't care about physical things, Martha. My meat is to do the will of my Father. I am the bread of life.*

We need to be reminded of this because our world puts so much emphasis on outer things. Here is just one example:

*physical appearance.* From the childhood story about the ugly duckling to commercials on television, American society says that appearance is everything. If we are not careful, we buy into it, forgetting that God's eyesight is different (1 Samuel 16:7). He looks at the heart!

Of course there is nothing wrong with trying to look nice. But do you remember one of the things that tempted Achan at the conquest of Jericho? It led to Israel's humiliating defeat at Ai and eventually to the destruction of Achan's entire family. He saw a "goodly Babylonian garment." (One version calls it a "beautiful coat.") This object appealed to his outer nature, and he apparently became so obsessed it eventually caused him to forget God's instructions. Overemphasis of physical things can do that.

Thirdly, from the story of Martha, we see that *by concentrating on the trivial, we miss out on the extraordinary.* In the movie *Dennis the Menace*, young Dennis' neighbor, Mr. Wilson, had a plant that he was convinced was going to win him all kinds of glory and recognition from the town's Garden Club. He owned a rare flower (called a Century Plant), that only blossomed for a few short seconds every century. The Wilsons had invited all of the city's influential citizens over to witness this important event. Everyone was seated in the backyard. At just the moment when the flower was to bloom, however, Dennis lived up to his nickname. He knocked over the food tables, creating a huge distraction. Everybody looked away from the plant to see what had happened and missed out on what they had come to see. By the time they turned back, the rare moment was over.

In the Bible, things of lesser importance draw Martha's attention away from Jesus. Mary, on the other hand, recognizes something that her sister forgot. Jesus would not always be in their company. He was on His way to Jerusalem; He would die soon. So while He was there, she stopped. She listened. She took advantage of an opportunity for spiritual growth.

Another difference in these two sisters, besides what they did, was their attitude. Martha complained; she had a pity party. Sure, she had a lot to do, but more than likely, those things were of her own choosing. Often, the things we complain about are things we have chosen to do. And usually the people who have the most to complain about are not the ones who complain!

Three doctors of divinity were sitting around one night discussing the characteristics of the ideal wife. The first gentleman said he thought Martha of Bethany filled the bill. The second gentleman said he would prefer her sister Mary. The third doctor said, "I think I would choose Martha before dinner . . . and Mary afterwards!"

Ideally, we need a little of both of these women in us. We all have roles to fulfill and responsibilities to meet. Certainly, we want to make our homes all they should be. But above everything, we should choose the better part and, like Mary, take time to sit at the feet of Jesus.

### Exercise

If you are like most women,
you have a tendency
to require too much of yourself.
Read Micah 6:8.
How refreshing!
What three simple things
does the Lord require?

## Scriptures

Matthew 6:21

Matthew 6:33

Luke 2:41-49

John 6:66-68

John 12:21

Acts 22:3

1 Thessalonians 5:17,18

# Chapter 9

# *Humor Helps*

*Reader's Digest*
is right.
Laughter IS
the best medicine.

# Humor Helps

Sarah had wanted a child all her life, but she was barren. By the time three men appeared on her doorstep in Genesis 18, I imagine she had given up on that dream. After all, she was 90 years old, and her husband was 100.

Still, the visitors—angels, it turned out—had some news for her. She was going to have a baby. Now, that would have been fantastic news 60 years earlier. At this point, however, I wonder just how thrilled Sarah was. (Someone has said, she probably thought, "Great! I will be the only one in the nursing home actually nursing.")

What did Sarah do? The Bible tells us she laughed. I wonder if maybe she laughed to keep from crying! That is what we have to do sometimes, you know.

Laughter is a great remedy for the stresses of modern-day living, according to counselors.

"Reality is sometimes not so pleasant," says Kay Parker, who works at an Alabama cancer center. "Humor is letting reality lay off for just a little while."

She compares it to moving a piece of furniture. "It gets heavy after a bit, and you need a short break. Once the break is over, you are ready to go again. It is the same way with stress. Taking a break from reality and thinking of something humorous can give you the rest you need. After you laugh, there is a period of relaxation."

Dr. Jaqueline Sales, a Brazilian physician in the northeastern city of Fortaleza, uses group laughter to treat patients who suffer from depression, stress, and diabetes. According to an article in a 2003 issue of American Spectator, Dr. Sales reported success from merely bringing patients together for paper fights and karaoke sessions. (American Spectator proposed she might do well to have them read from the Congressional Record.)

Even the Pentagon is on board, encouraging military families to use laughter as a way to deal with stresses related to the war in Iraq. Retired Army Colonel James "Scotty" Scott, certified by a group called the World Laughter Tour in Ohio, directs sessions that he believes will prevent "hardening of the attitudes."

(By the way, the founder and chief executive of the World Laughter Tour, psychologist Steve Wilson, calls himself "Cheerman of the Bored.")

The program encourages acting silly—waddling like a penguin, laughing drills, etc. The more ridiculous, the better, experts claim.

A merry heart maketh a cheerful countenance...

— *Proverbs* 15:13 (KJV)

Parker's motto with her cancer patients, in fact, is: *It helps to be crazy; it keeps you from going insane.*

Does God have a sense of humor? Sure, He does. If you do not think so, just visit a zoo sometime and see all the funny animals He created. Or for that matter, look in the mirror first thing in the morning! God is the one who made us able to laugh. He knows it is good for us.

Proverbs 15:15 says, "A merry heart hath a continual feast." A continual feast—wow! How many of us tend to eat when we get stressed? A pint of chocolate chip ice cream or a king-sized candy bar. (My sister once sent me a funny E-mail asking, "How much Healthy Choice ice cream can I eat before it's no longer a healthy choice?")

Here is something we can chow down on that does not have any calories: laughter.

Proverbs 17:22 says, "A merry heart doeth good like a medicine." A cure-all? No, but it is as close to it as anything you can buy in a pharmacy.

## Excuse Me for a Moment While I Scream

In his book, *Never Lick A Frozen Flagpole,* Marvin Phillips tells of a university in the northeast that has a "scream break" every afternoon at 2:00. They supposedly love to surprise visitors on campus who are not aware of the tradition, he says. Students may be relaxing outdoors, walking back from the library, or in their dorm rooms studying, but when the clock strikes two, everybody stands up and screams at the top of their lungs.

Not a bad way to relieve tension.

If you are not a screamer, Phillips suggests taking a laughter break or a five-minute getaway. Close your eyes and, in your mind, go to a calm setting faraway. Imagine the reaction you would get when your kids call you for something and you reply, "Not now. I am on vacation!"

## Exercise

A movie, a television show, or a comic strip that can always make me laugh is:

_____

_____

_____

_____

Some people who never fail to bring a smile to my face are:

_____

_____

_____

_____

A funny incident from the past that I will never forget is:

_____

_____

_____

_____

_____

_____

## Exercise

Some suggestions when it comes to humor:

1. As much as possible, keep your focus on the funny side of life. Fill your mind with good things (1 Thessalonians 5:21; Philippians 4:8).
2. Keep a running list of blessings (Colossians 3:15).
3. Start a file folder of humorous quotes, clippings, and cartoons.
4. Read humorous books.
5. Write down funny things your kids say and do.
6. Ask your older relatives about funny things they remember happening.

### Scriptures

Psalm 118:24

Psalm 144:15

Psalm 146:5

Proverbs 15:13

Proverbs 15:15

Proverbs 17:22

James 5:13

# Chapter 10

# *Mirror, Mirror, On The Wall*

*Drop thy still dews of quietness*
*till all our strivings cease.*
*Take from our souls the*
*strain and stress*
*And let our ordered lives confess*
*the beauty of thy peace.*

*— From "Dear Lord and Father of Mankind"*
*John Greenleaf Whittier*

# "Mirror, Mirror, On The Wall . . ."

"No female ever thinks she looks good enough."

So says one of the characters in Cassandra King's novel, *The Same Sweet Girls.* As proof, the character tells her friends about a study conducted about college students:

> See, they got a group of males and a group of females to rank themselves for their attractiveness, how they saw themselves. Then they got a panel of judges, folks who judged beauty contests, modeling agencies, stuff like that, to rank them. When they compared the numbers, all the males ranked themselves higher than the judges did. And, no surprise — without exception, the females ranked themselves lower.

Now I am not sure if such research is legitimate, or something Ms. King merely invented for literary purposes. One thing, however, is certain: females struggle with confidence issues. (Not exclusively, of course; I realize men can — and do — have low self-esteem as well. But how many males routinely come home from a dinner party comparing what they wore to the other guys in attendance? Or else determined to begin redecorating their homes immediately?)

Let us face it, we gals constantly compare ourselves to others. And I am convinced that part of today's stress-filled, pressure cooker lives are based on our efforts to keep pace with what we view as the competition.

Pick up a copy of your typical woman's magazine. What do you see inside? Perfection. Females with great hairstyles and no wrinkles. Their nails are done, their homes are fashionable (not to mention spotless). We look at that, and then look at ourselves, and guess what? We do not measure up. And it is frustrating. We end up trying to be all that the world says we should be to be successful, but we never achieve it. So we are stressed out from trying and disheartened from failure.

When it comes to ladies' magazines, I have one word for you: air brushed! I applaud the actress Jamie Curtis who, a few years back, allowed herself to be photographed "as is." (No touch-ups permitted.) It is about time Hollywood stopped perpetuating myths of perfection which drive American women to plastic surgery, eating disorders, or depression.

Our self-confidence should come not from our mirror but from God. We are special because of who our Father is, so we should hold our heads up high. We should feel good about ourselves and not worry if we do not have all that the world tells us we need to be beautiful.

Peter, in the third chapter of his first epistle, says that true beauty comes from a gentle and quiet spirit, which is precious in the sight of God.

## EXERCISE
### Beauty Treatment

❖ The next time you are tempted to launch into a body comparison, read Psalm 139:14. In what ways are you "wonderfully" made? List some things you really like about your appearance. (Come on now, this is no time to be modest!)

❖ A preacher who had performed over 200 weddings once said that he had never seen an ugly bride! Is there a connection between happiness and beauty? Make a concentrated effort to choose to be happy and see if it makes a difference. (For fun, drag out one of your old wedding pictures, dust if off and display it in a pretty frame somewhere in your home. Challenge yourself to rediscover that radiance!)

❖ Make a list of the things you read and watch on TV for the next few days. Examine these in light of what is "lovely" in the sight of God (Philippians 4:8). Remember, what you look at has a lot to do with what you look like!

❖ Read Romans 12:2 in a modern translation. List some of the ways the world around us constantly tries to "squeeze us into its mold."

❖ Think of an example of something someone did in the past that made you feel good about yourself. Look for things you can do to build self-esteem in those around you.

## EXERCISE
### Men Walk, Women Talk

According to an article in the *USA Today* newspaper, males and females have different mechanisms for coping with anger. Men let off steam by getting outdoors and doing something physical (example: chopping wood). Women, on the other hand, tend to want to talk things over with a girlfriend.

Now, talking can be good, but when it comes to reducing the stress in our lives, we gals might do well to imitate the menfolk and exercise something more than just our vocal chords.

Regular physical activity has been proven to be not only good for the body and heart, but for the spirit and soul as well.

Schedule some exercise in your busy life. Begin with something small and manageable. Walk ten minutes in your neighborhood in the late afternoon or early evening. Go to a local park where you can enjoy the beauties of nature while you jog. Take the stairs instead of an elevator whenever possible.

Gradually build up your level of activity. Increase the time in small increments. Move on to more strenuous pursuits, if desired.

If you must, get a friend to walk or work out with you. After all, we want to keep those vocal chords in shape, too, right?

## Scriptures

Ruth 3:11

1 Samuel 16:7

Proverbs 31:30

Isaiah 3:18-24

Philippians 4:8

1 Peter 3:3,4

1 Timothy 2:9,10

# Chapter 11
## *Spontaneity*

*"Spontaneity is the quality of being able to do something just because you feel like it at the moment, of trusting your instincts, of taking yourself by surprise and snatching from the clutches of your well-organized routine a bit of unscheduled pleasure."*

# Spontaneity

The dictionary defines *spontaneity* as "impetuous, unplanned; arising from a momentary impulse, acting under the spirit of the moment."

There is nothing like spontaneity to relieve the stresses and pressures of day-to-day life.

I can remember times, home-bound with four little ones and about ready to pull my hair out, when my husband would come in and say—on the spur of the moment—"Let's go get ice cream" or "Let's go to the park." (Or even better, "Let me take the kids to the park or to get ice-cream!")

An unexpected change in routine was wonderful—just what we all needed.

When pressure builds up, relieve tension by doing something fun and out-of-the-ordinary with those closest to you.

One mom told me that on rare occasions when her children are bursting with pent-up energy, she temporarily suspends the "No Jumping on the Bed" rule. She even joins the kiddos in bouncing up and down, sock-footed, on a mattress. Now that is a memory in the making, to be sure!

Let's say it is a rainy day when children are stuck indoors, and the noise level in your house has you spinning. Instead of continually shushing everyone, why not grant permission—even encourage—your preschoolers to be loud? Pass out pots, pans, and wooden spoons, and lead a parade through the house!

ın *Make Memories for Your Children,* Hermaline Sullivan writes the following:

> To be friends with your children, to laugh and run and dance with your children is making memories. I hope that when I am very old, one of my children will remind me of the days when I used to dance in the front room with the broom. I hope they will be able to say, "Mother mostly always stopped to read a story," or "My mother was a very funny and laughing mother. Remember the picnics, remember the sea, remember the candy party and tea and toast we used to have on a rainy afternoon?"
>
> I shudder to think of my children remembering how clean their house always was. Or how they always had to wear a spanking clean shirt to the grocery store. Wouldn't it be terrible if my children remembered simply that I wouldn't allow them to build a tent in the front room?

An old *Reader's Digest* story tells of a woman who allowed her children and their friends to work on projects in the kitchen while she cooked dinner. There was chatter and fun around the well-worn table, and occasionally smidgens of paint and clay even found their way into the food.

Years later, her college-age son brought an old friend home for dinner. "I always loved coming to your house, Mrs. Spencer," he said, giving her a big hug. "We had lots of laughs—and there was Play-Doh in the soup!"

# From The Mother's Almanac

Every day you and your husband add a little more to your child's legacy, and money is the least of it.

It's the time you spend with him and the way you spend it that determines the richness of his heritage. The summer walks may seem a bother, the fishing trip too much, but they set the mood for talking—a habit once set that can never be lost.

The adventures you offer should be frequent and varied, with good planning for the special ones and spontaneity for the rest. Just as you prepare for his outing, so must he help you prepare for the family celebrations. When you let your child make a pecan pie for Thanksgiving or arrange the flowers for company dinner, you're giving him memories for a lifetime. Which is as it should be. They'll be your memories, too.

—By Marguerite Kelly and Elia Parsons

## EXERCISE

### Acting Under
### The Spirit of the Moment

Be spontaneous with your spouse this week. Plan something romantic. "Kidnap" him for lunch. Put the kids to bed early and serve a candlelight meal in your bedroom—dressed in your finest lingerie!

Remember you are the mood-setter for your family. Copy the statement *If Mama ain't happy, ain't nobody happy* onto a piece of paper and stick it on your refrigerator as a reminder.

Plan a 30-minute date this week with each of your children separately. If they are young, you might want to do one of the following:

— go for a long walk

— swing

— make a tent under the dining room table

— play dress-up

If they are older, let *them* suggest an outing. (Be sure it is one that does not involve money!)

Do something unexpected for a parent.

Do something unexpected for a friend.

Do something for yourself, too!

## Scriptures

Psalm 37:4

Psalm 90:14

Psalm 116:7

Isaiah 32:18

Mark 2:2-4

Mark 10:14

John 21:4-12

# Chapter 12

# *Don't Be A Pheidippides*

"*I've been livin'*
*in fast forward.*
*Now I need to*
*rewind real slow.*"

— *Kenny Chesney*

REWIND

## Don't Be a Pheidippides

All of us, I imagine, have heard of marathons. But do you know how the race got its name?

Back in 490 B.C., the Greeks were at war with the Persians. Persian soldiers had destroyed the Greek city of Eretria and were on the march again toward the plain of Marathon. A Greek soldier named Pheidippides ran from Athens to Sparta—24 hard miles without stopping—to take the news. But as soon as he arrived and delivered his message, he dropped dead from exhaustion. Today, the famous marathon race commemorates his accomplishment.

Perhaps you have run a marathon. Even if you have not, you likely race around constantly in an "every-day-a-thon"!

Rick Atchley tells about a friend who worked a full-time job, a part-time job, and also attended graduate school. On top of that, he was married and had two children. One Sunday morning, as he stood up to teach a Bible class, he apologized for his rather haggard appearance. "I'm tired," he explained. "I think I have been tired ever since the eighth grade!"

Are you tired?

When one of our sons was a little boy, he had one speed, and that was fast. He went ninety to nothing, non-stop, whenever he was awake. Occasionally, though (this happened several times), he would be sick and run a high fever for about 24 hours. I would put him to bed, and he would sleep straight through, then wake up feeling fine. I always said his body did that so he would be forced to get some rest.

In Greece, a monastery sits high on a cliff, several hundred feet in the air. The only way to reach it is to climb into a basket, which is suspended from a rope. Monks on the cliff then tug with all their strength and pull the basket up to the top. (How would you like a ride like that?)

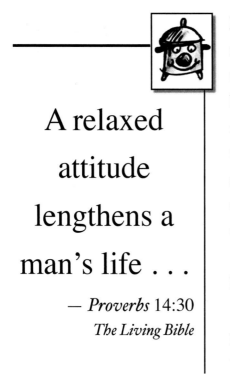

A relaxed attitude lengthens a man's life . . .

— *Proverbs* 14:30
*The Living Bible*

One tourist, about halfway up, became rather nervous when he noticed that the rope by which the basket was suspended was rather old and frayed. In a trembling voice, he asked a fellow passenger just how often the monks changed the rope.

The reply? "Whenever it breaks, I guess."

That is not a very good philosophy, is it? Some things we need to take care of before a break occurs.

Take time to rest. Your body needs it, and so does your soul.

## Learning to Simplify

It has been said that most men have six items, maximum, in their bathrooms.

Women, on the average, have 437! (None of which their husbands can even identify!)

Okay, face it. We are a bit more complicated than males.

I love the his/her instructions for Automated Teller Machines which made the rounds on the Internet a while back:

**HIS:**
1. Pull up to ATM.
2. Insert card.
3. Enter PIN.
4. Take cash, card, and receipt.
5. Drive away.

**HERS:**
1. Pull up to ATM.
2. Back up and move forward to get closer.
3. Shut off engine.
4. Put keys in purse.
5. Get out of car because you are still too far away.
6. Hunt for card in purse.
7. Insert card.
8. Hunt in purse for grocery receipt with PIN.
9. Enter PIN.

10. Study instructions.

11. Hit CANCEL button.

12. Re-enter correct PIN.

13. Check balance.

14. Look in purse for pen.

15. Look for envelope.

16. Make out deposit slip.

17. Endorse check.

18. Make deposit.

19. Study instructions.

20. Make cash withdrawal.

21. Get in car.

22. Check makeup.

23. Start pulling away.

24. Stop.

25. Back up to machine.

26. Get out of car.

27. Take card and receipt.

28. Get back in car.

29. Enter deposit and withdrawal in checkbook.

30. Put car in reverse.

31. Put car in drive.

32. Drive three miles.

33. Release parking brake.

So we *are* complicated. But that does not mean *life* has to be complicated.

Simplicity is defined as *"freedom from complications, freedom from pretense. Not complex, concerned only with fundamentals."*

Do these words describe your life?

## "Hifalutin" Lifestyles

I have in my files a game that is always fun to play. Actually, it is a set of famous sayings, but they are listed in "hifalutin terms." For example, "It is fruitless to become lachrymose because of scattered lacteal liquid." That is a fancy way for saying: "Don't cry over spilt milk." Another famous saying put in hifalutin terms is: "Refrain from detonating the missile until the opaque colorless parts of the visual organ are in evidence," which means, "Don't shoot until you see the whites of their eyes." Often, folks have a hard time figuring out what the words on the game sheet really mean because the language is so involved.

The original quotations are much briefer . . . and much easier to understand. Sometimes I think our lives are like the sentences on this game: they have become all hifalutin. We keep adding more and more, keep making things more elaborate, and it is killing us. What is the solution? Simplify.

## Exercise

Here are some practical suggestions:

1. Learn to be content (Philippians 4:11; 1 Timothy 6:8; Hebrews 13:5).

2. Start the day right. The key to getting a good start is to do everything possible the night before to prepare. Get a coffee maker that can be timed to start brewing when you wake up. Decide in advance what you are going to wear, and iron it if necessary. Kids can set the table with cereal, bowls, spoons, everything but the milk. Get them in the habit of gathering their things up before going to bed. Set anything that is to be carried out with you—dry cleaning, book packs, etc.—by the door. Always put keys in the same place. (Studies show that the average adult spends 16 hours a year searching for lost keys!)

3. De-clutter your home. "Every possession you buy requires tending," says Don Aslett, author of *Clutter's Last Stand*. "Every chair, blouse, stationary bike, candlestick must be dusted, guarded, stored, or repaired. Freeing yourself from unnecessary possessions frees up time."

Clutter experts suggest you start small, perhaps cleaning out one drawer or one shelf a day. If something is broken, fix it or toss it out. If it does not fit, alter it or give it away.

Train yourself and your family not to put anything down for just now. Do not leave jackets on chairs or glasses in the sink—put them away where they belong.

4. Learn to say no.

5. Do not save pennies and waste hours. Most of us are taught to watch money but not to value time, says Andrea Van Steenhouse, author of *A Woman's Guide To A Simpler Life*. As a result, we may not even think about how much irreplaceable time we waste to save a few pennies. Is it worth it to wander through a giant warehouse searching for picture hangers when we could find them immediately at a neighborhood hardware store?

6. Let others help. Insist that others help. Give your kids chores to do. They may not quite meet your expectations, but realize that a poorly made bed is better than one left unmade.

7. Turn off the television more. Americans average 16 hours a week watching TV, making it our nation's dominant leisure activity.

8. Stop telephone interruptions. Ask telemarketers to take you off their lists. "Legally, solicitors have to stop," says Jeff Davidson, author of *The Joy of Simple Living*. You may also want to cancel call waiting or turn phones off during meals.

9. Practice doing nothing. Adam and Eve had a lot to do—caring for the flowers and vegetables, naming animals—but they still took time to walk in the garden. (Of course, come to think of it, they did not have to do laundry, did they?)

10. Accept God's rest. Memorize Matthew 11:28-30.

## Scriptures

Genesis 27:46

Deuteronomy 25:17,18

Judges 4:21

2 Samuel 17:1,2

Habakkuk 2:13

1 Timothy 6:8

Hebrews 12:1

# Chapter 13

# *The Art of Doing Nothing*

### Slow Me Down, Lord

*Slow me down, Lord! Ease the pounding of my heart by the quieting of my mind. Steady my hurried pace with a vision of the eternal reach of time. Give me, amidst the confusion of my day, the calmness of the everlasting hills. Break the tension of my nerves and muscles with the soothing music of the singing streams that live in my memory. Help me to know the magical restorative power of sleep. Teach me the art of taking minute vacations, of slowing down to look at a flower, to chat with a friend, to pat a dog, to read a few lines from a good book. Remind me each day of the fable of the hare and the tortoise, that I may know that the race is not always to the swift; that there is more to life than increasing its speed. Let me look upward into the branches of the towering oak, and know that it grew slowly and well. Slow me down, Lord, and inspire me to send my roots deep into the soil of life's enduring values, that I may grow toward the stars of my greatest destiny. Amen.*

*— Anonymous*

## The Art of Doing Nothing

Lightning had struck an old farmer's ramshackle shed and saved him the trouble of tearing it down. Rain had rinsed the mud off his truck and saved him the trouble of washing it. He was sitting on his front porch one day and someone asked him what he was doing. "Waiting for an earthquake to come along," he said, "to shake my potatoes out of the ground!"

That fellow's tendency was to do nothing. We, on the other hand, try to do too much, and in the process we wear ourselves out. This is often the case with regard to spiritual matters.

Now, please do not get me wrong. Of course, there are things we need to do as Christians. Ephesians says we were created for good works; other scriptures attest to the fact that the world is going to know us by the things we do, and Revelation 20:12 tells that we will be judged according to the words written in these books.

Yet many times, I am afraid, we rush around and stress ourselves out trying to work our way to heaven.

Am I doing enough? I ought to be doing more!

Am I saved? Well, I hope so. Maybe if I do this, and this, and this . . . .

The parable of the workers in Matthew 20 gives tremendous insight into the attitude we should have towards our salvation. Notice verses 1-15:

For the kingdom of heaven is like a landowner who went out early in the morning to hire laborers for his vineyard. Now when he had agreed with the laborers for a denarius a day, he sent them into his vineyard. And he went out about the third hour and saw others standing idle in the marketplace, and said to them, You also go into the vineyard, and whatever is right I will give you. So they went. Again he went out about the sixth and the ninth hour, and did likewise. And about the eleventh hour he went out and found others standing idle, and said to them, Why have you been standing here idle all day? They said to him, Because no one hired us. He said to them, You also go into the vineyard, and whatever is right you will receive. So when evening had come, the owner of the vineyard said to his steward, Call the laborers and give them their wages, beginning with the last to the first. And when those came who were hired about the eleventh hour, they each received a denarius. But when the first came, they supposed that they would receive more; and they likewise received each a denarius.

And when they had received it, they complained against the landowner, saying, These last men have worked only one hour, and you made them equal to us who have borne the burden and the heat of the day. But he answered one of them and said, Friend, I am doing you no wrong. Did you not agree with me for a denarius? Take what is yours and go your way.

I wish to give to this last man the same as to you. Is it not lawful for me to do what I wish with my own things? Or is your eye evil because I am good?

I will confess this story used to cause me all kinds of problems. My initial reaction upon hearing it was always: That is not fair! On the surface, it does not seem to be, does it? It goes against everything we have ever been taught. You know, "An honest day's pay for an honest day's work."

The problem is that we spend too much time focusing on the wrong characters and miss the point. In Jesus' parables, not every little detail has a lesson for us; often there is just one overriding teaching.

So forget about the fellows who worked three,

> He maketh me to lie down in green pastures: he leadeth me beside the still waters.
>
> — *Psalm* 23:2 (KJV)

six, nine, and twelve hours. Concentrate on the guy who worked one measly hour and was paid for a full day! (I call him the "lazy bum." Maybe I am wrong, but I do not think he was so diligent he came in with only one hour to go and ended up picking as many grapes as anybody else and really impressing the foreman. No, the idea seems to be, he stood around, goofing off in the marketplace right in the middle of harvest season when there were plenty of jobs available if one wanted to work!)

Now, I know, most of us cannot really relate to him. We identify more with the early-riser, the full-day worker. A good, responsible employee. Doing what is expected of us.

But the point of the story is we are not like that at all. This whole parable is about grace and how God, in His goodness, gives us what we do not deserve.

None of us gets paid according to merit because none of us comes anywhere close to satisfying God's requirements for a perfect life. What does Romans 3:23 say? "All have sinned and fallen short of God's glory." According to Psalm 14:3, "[N]one are righteous, no, not one." If we were paid on the basis of what is fair, we would all end up lost because the Bible tells us even when we have done everything we should, we are still unprofitable servants.

When you think about this bum who worked a mere sixty minutes and was given a full day's salary, your focus automatically shifts to where it should be: on the boss. Surely this has to be the most generous master in the world!

That is our God.

What is the point? We do not need to tally up points in regards to our salvation; it is not a debit/credit situation. Remember the prodigal son who wanted to come back as a servant, to work and earn his way? The father would not permit it. He welcomed him as a son.

As God's children, we are not working to earn a paycheck. We work out of gratitude, out of love for a kind and generous master. And that makes all the difference in the world.

## Who Moved My Pole?

A recent *Reader's Digest* tells the story of a woman who was riding a crowded city bus one day. She noticed that the young man who was standing across from her, holding onto the same pole, kept staring at her. Eventually, he leaned over and said, "Excuse me, ma'am, this is my stop."

Since she was not blocking his way, she was confused. "Well, go ahead," she said.

"You don't understand," he replied. "This is also my pole. I just bought it at the hardware store to hold up my shower curtain!"

Are we holding onto the wrong things in life—things that are not even permanent and secure?

We need to hold onto the Lord, whom we are told changes not (Malachi 3:6).

No matter what upheavals occur around us, nothing can shake or move Him.

As Psalm 46:2 says, "Therefore we will not fear, even though the earth be removed, and though the mountains be carried into the midst of the sea."

## EXERCISE
## Tally Your Time

We are all busy, no doubt about it. But what do we really do? How much of our time do we spend on unimportant things?

To help yourself get a true picture, try charting your actions for a 72-hour period. Record everything you do, even talking on the phone or going shopping.

When you tally it all up, you may be surprised at just where your time really goes.

❖ How much is spent with loved ones?

❖ How much is spent with the Lord?

❖ How much is spent helping others?

❖ How much is spent on self?

Anne Ortlund, in her book *Disciplines of the Beautiful Woman,* vows never to devote more than 1/22 of her time to physical appearance. On the surface that appears to be an odd fraction. How did she arrive at that? I wondered. Apparently, she noted the qualities of the worthy woman listed in Proverbs 31. Of the 22 attributes given, only one has to do with good looks!

Using that as her basis, therefore, Ortlund proportions this rather small allotment to outer concerns, and the rest to spiritual development: becoming wiser, kinder, more godly, and hard-working.

How do you measure up to this quotient?

Do you spend an hour a day—or more—on your hair, nails, makeup, wardrobe, physical fitness? Contrast this with the time you spend maintaining and promoting inner beauty. For most of us, the discrepancy is substantial.

## Scriptures

Psalm 23:2

Habakkuk 1:5

Romans 6:18

Romans 8:28

Ephesians 2:8,9

Philippians 4:11

1 Timothy 6:6

# CONCLUSION

I realize I am probably guilty of doing the very thing I have told you not to do! This book has been a quick read. (My rationale, of course, was that you would think you didn't have time to read something long and involved!) Still, I know I have run the risk of leaving you feeling unprepared to make major changes. Hopefully, you have not come away thinking, "Well, that did not help one bit!"

We have a tendency to be like the little girl who went fishing one day with her daddy. They sat quietly on the pier for awhile. After about ten minutes, she jumped up and announced she was ready to quit and go home.

"But, why?" her father asked. "We just got here."

"I don't care," the little girl replied, "I just can't seem to get waited on!"

We all want instant results. We become discouraged if things do not happen right away.

Unfortunately, there are not any quick fixes when it comes to dealing with stress. In fact, most any time we attempt to alter our lives, it is going to be a slow and deliberate process.

So do not give up if things in your world spiral out of control at times. The fast pace probably is not going to go away any time soon.

But just because we live in a pressure cooker world does not mean we have to stay all steamed up and spew out the top.

We can turn our setting down to LOW.

We can learn to simmer in God's love and blessings.

# REFLECTIONS